SPECIAL DAYS
THROUGHOUT
THE YEAR

50 Ready-to-Use Activities
for Grades 3–9

SPECIAL DAYS THROUGHOUT THE YEAR

50 Ready-to-Use Activities for Grades 3–9

Audrey J. Adair

Illustrated by Leah Solsrud

MUSIC CURRICULUM ACTIVITIES LIBRARY

Parker Publishing Company, Inc.
West Nyack, N.Y.

© 1987 *by*

PARKER PUBLISHING COMPANY, INC.

West Nyack, N.Y.

10 9 8 7 6 5 4 3 2

Library of Congress Cataloging-in-Publication Data

Adair, Audrey J.
  Special days throughout the year.

  (Music curriculum activities library ; unit 6)
    1. School music—Instruction and study.   2. Holidays—
United States.   I. Title.   II. Series: Adair, Audrey J.,
              Music curriculum activities library ;
unit 6.
MT10.A14   1987   unit 6   372.8'7 s [372.8'7]   87-8839

ISBN 0-13-826421-X

Printed in the United States of America

About the Author

Audrey J. Adair has taught music at all levels in the Houston, Texas, and Dade County, Florida, public schools. She has served as a music consultant, music specialist, general music instructor, choir director, and classroom teacher. In addition, she has written a series of musical programs for assemblies and holiday events, conducted music workshops, organized music programs for the community, established glee club organizations, and done specialization work with gifted and special needs students. Currently, she directs and coordinates children's choirs, performs as soloist with flute as well as voice, and composes sacred music.

Mrs. Adair received her B.A. in Music Education from St. Olaf College in Northfield, Minnesota, and has done graduate work at the University of Houston and Florida Atlantic University in Fort Lauderdale. She is also the author of *Ready-to-Use Music Activities Kit* (Parker Publishing Company), a resource containing over 200 reproducible worksheets to teach basic music skills and concepts.

About the *Library*

The *Music Curriculum Activities Library* was developed for you, the busy classroom teacher and music specialist, to provide a variety of interesting, well-rounded, step-by-step activities ready for use in your music classroom. The *Library*'s seven carefully planned Units combine imagination, motivation, and student involvement to make learning as exciting as going on a field trip and as easy as listening to music.

The units of the *Music Curriculum Activities Library* are designed to be used separately or in conjunction with each other. Each Unit contains 50 *all new* ready-to-use music activity sheets that can be reproduced as many times as needed for use by individual students. These 350 illustrated, easy-to-read activities will turn even your most reluctant students into eager learners. Each Unit offers a wealth of information on the following topics:

Unit 1: *Basic Music Theory* develops an understanding of the basic elements of melody, rhythm, harmony, and dynamics.

Unit 2: *Reading and Writing Music* provides a source of reinforcement and instills confidence in the beginner performer through a wide range of note-reading and writing activities in the treble clef, bass clef, and in the clef of one's own instrument.

Unit 3: *Types of Musical Form and Composition* gives the student the foundation needed to enjoy worthwhile music by becoming acquainted with a wide variety of styles and representative works.

Unit 4: *Musical Instruments and the Voice* provides knowledge of and insight into the characteristic sounds of band, orchestra, folk instruments, and the voice.

Unit 5: *Great Composers and Their Music* familiarizes the student with some of the foremost composers of the past and present and their music; and cultivates an early taste for good music.

Unit 6: *Special Days Throughout the Year* offers the student well-illustrated, music-related activities that stimulate interest and discussion about music through holidays and special occasions for the entire school year.

Unit 7: *Musicians in Action* helps the student examine music as a pastime or for a career by exploring daily encounters with music and the skills, duties, environment, and requirements of a variety of careers in music.

How to Use the *Library*

The activities in each Unit of the *Library* may be sequenced and developed in different ways. The general teacher may want to use one activity after the other, while the music specialist may prefer to use the activities in conjunction with the sequencing of the music curriculum. Teachers with special or individualized needs may select activities from various Units and use them over and over before actually introducing new material.

Let's take a closer look at how you can use the *Music Curriculum Activities Library* in your particular classroom situation:

...For THE MUSIC TEACHER who is accountable for teaching classes at many grade levels, there is a wide range of activities with varying degrees of difficulty. The activity sheets are ideal to strengthen and review skills and concepts suitable for the general music class.

...For THE NEW TEACHER STARTING A GENERAL MUSIC CLASS, these fun-filled activities will provide a well-balanced, concrete core program.

...For THE SPECIALIZED TEACHER who needs to set definite teaching goals, these activities offer a wealth of information about certain areas of music, such as career awareness, composers, and musical forms.

...For THE BAND AND CHOIR DIRECTOR, these activity sheets are a valuable resource to explore band, orchestra, and folk instruments, along with the singing voice.

...For THE PRIVATE MUSIC TEACHER who wants to sharpen and improve students' note reading skills, the *Library* offers ample homework assignments to give students the additional practice they need. There are many activity sheets using the clef of one's instrument and theory pages with illustrations of the keyboard.

...For THE MUSIC CONSULTANT using any one of the units, there are plenty of activities specifically correlated to the various areas of music providing reinforcement of learning. The activity sheets are suitable for class adoption in correlation with any music book series.

...For THE THEORY TEACHER, there are activities to show the students that music analysis is fun and easy.

...For THE TEACHER WHO NEEDS AN ADEQUATE MEANS OF EVALUATING STUDENT PROGRESS, there are fact-filled activities ideal for diagnostic purposes. A space is provided on each sheet for a score to be given.

. . . For THE CLASSROOM TEACHER with little or no musical background, the *Library* offers effective teaching with the flexibility of the seven units. All that has to be done is to decide on the music skill or concept to be taught and then duplicate the necessary number of copies. Even the answers can be duplicated for self-checking.

. . . For THE SUBSTITUTE TEACHER, these sheets are ideal for seatwork assignments because the directions are generally self-explanatory with minimal supervision required.

. . . For THE INSTRUCTOR OF GIFTED STUDENTS, the activities may be used for any type of independent, individualized instruction and learning centers. When used in an individualized fashion, the gifted student has an opportunity to pursue music learning at his or her own pace.

. . . For THE TEACHER OF SPECIAL EDUCATION, even the disadvantaged and remedial student can get in on the fun. Each concept or skill will be mastered as any lesson may be repeated or reinforced with another activity. Some of these activity sheets are designed to provide success for students who have difficulty in other subject areas.

. . . For the INDIVIDUAL who desires to broaden and expand his or her own knowledge and interest in music, each Unit provides 50 activities to help enjoy music.

The *Music Curriculum Activities Library* is ideally a teacher's program because a minimum of planning is required. A quick glance at the Contents in each Unit reveals the titles of all the activity sheets, the ability level necessary to use them, and the skills involved for each student. Little knowledge of music is generally needed to introduce the lessons, and extensive preparation is seldom necessary. You will, of course, want to read through the activity before presenting it to the class. In cases where you need to give information about the activity, two different approaches might be considered. (1) Use the activity as a basis for a guided discussion before completing the activity to achieve the desired results, or (2) Use the activity as a foundation for a lesson plan and then follow up by completing the activity. Either one of these approaches will enhance your own and your students' confidence and, by incorporating a listening or performing experience with this directed study, the students will have a well-rounded daily lesson.

All activity sheets throughout the *Library* have the same format. They are presented in an uncluttered, easy-to-read fashion, with self-explanatory directions. You need no extra materials or equipment, except for an occasional pair of scissors. The classroom or resource area should, however, contain a few reference books, such as song books or music series' books, encyclopedias, reference books about composers, a dictionary, music dictionary or glossary, and so on, so that while working on certain activities the student has easy access to resource books. Then, you simply need to duplicate the activity sheet as many

times as needed and give a copy to each student. Even paper grading can be kept
to a minimum by reproducing the answer key for self-checking.

The collection of activities includes practice in classifying, matching, listing,
researching, naming, drawing, decoding, identifying, doing picture or crossword
puzzles, anagrams, word searches, musical word squares, and much much more.

These materials may be used successfully with students in grades 3 and up.
The activities and artwork are intentionally structured to appeal to a wide range
of ages. For this reason, no grade-level references appear on the activity sheets
so that you can use them in a variety of classroom settings, although suggested
ability levels (beginner, intermediate, advanced) appear in the Contents.

The potential uses for the *Library* for any musical purpose (or even inter-
disciplinary study) are countless. Why? Because these activities allow you to in-
struct an entire class, a smaller group within the classroom, or individual
students. While you are actively engaged in teaching one group of students, the
activity sheets may be completed by another group. In any kind of classroom
setting, even with the gifted music student or the remedial child, no student
needs to sit idle. Now you will have more time for individual instruction.

The Units may be used in a comprehensive music skills program, in an enrich-
ment program, or even in a remedial program. The *Library* is perfect for building
a comprehensive musicianship program, improving basic music skills, teaching
career awareness, building music vocabulary, exploring instruments, developing
good taste in listening to music, appreciating different types of music, creating a
positive learning environment, and providing growing confidence in the performer.

What Each Unit Offers You

A quick examination of the **Contents** will reveal a well balanced curriculum. Included are the titles of all activities, the level of difficulty, and the skill involved. The exception to this is Unit 6, where the date and special day, rather than the skill, are listed with the title of each activity.

Each of the **50 reproducible activity sheets** generally presents a single idea, with a consistent format and easy-to-follow directions on how to do the activity, along with a sufficient amount of material to enable the student to become proficient through independent and self-directed work. Because each activity has but one single behavioral objective, mastery of each skill builds confidence that allows the learner to continue progressively toward a more complete understanding of the structure of music, appreciation of music, and its uses. The activity sheets are just the right length, too, designed to be completed within a class period.

The **Progress Chart** provides a uniform, objective method of determining what skills have been mastered. With the aid of this chart, you will be able to keep track of goals, set priorities, organize daily and weekly lesson plans, and track assignments. The Progress Chart lists each activity and skill involved, and has a space for individual names or classes to be recorded and checked when each activity and skill is complete. The Progress Chart is ideal for accurate record keeping. It provides a quick, sure method for you to determine each individual student's achievements or weaknesses.

Use the **Teacher's Guide** for practical guidance on how the particular Unit will work for you. An easy effective learning system, this guide provides background information and reveals new techniques for teaching the Unit.

Throughout the *Library*, each **Answer Key** is designed with a well-thought-out system for checking students' answers. While some activities are self-checking without the use of the Answer Key, other activities can easily be student corrected, too, by simply duplicating the answer page and cutting apart the answers by activity number.

The **Self-Improvement Chart** provides the student with a self-assessment system that links curriculum goals with individual goals. By means of an appraisal checklist, the chart gives the student and teacher alike the key to finding individual talent. It also measures accountability. Included in the chart are (1) a method for recording goals and acquired music skills; (2) a log for attendance at special music events; (3) a music and instrument check-out record; (4) a log for extra credit activities and music projects; (5) a record of special music recognition awards, incentive badges, Music Share-a-Grams, Return-a-Grams; and (6) a record of music progress.

These specific features of the chart will help you:

- Provide a uniform, objective method of determining rewards for students.
- Assess future curriculum needs by organizing long-term information on student performance.
- Foster understanding of why students did or did not qualify for additional merit.
- Motivate students by giving them feedback on ways for self-improvement.
- Assist students in making statements of their own desires and intentions for learning, and in checking progress toward their goals.

The **Music Share-a-Gram** is a personalized progress report addressed to the parent and created to show the unique qualities of the individual child. It allows you to pinpoint areas of success and tell parents what they need to know about their child. The Music Share-a-Gram evaluates twelve important abilities and personal traits with ratings from exceptional to unsatisfactory, which you might want to discuss with students to solicit their reaction. For example, you might use these ratings as a basis for selecting a student to attend the gifted program in music. This form is designed to be sent with or without the Return-a-Gram, and may be hand-delivered by the student or sent through the mail. For easy record keeping, make a copy of the Gram and attach it to the back of the Student Record Profile Chart.

The **Return-a-Gram** is designed to accompany the Music Share-a-Gram and is sent to the parent on special occasions. When a reply is not expected or necessary, simply detach the Return-a-Gram before sending the Share-a-Gram. This form encourages feedback from the parent and even allows the parent to arrange for a parent-teacher conference. Both Grams are printed on the same page and are self-explanatory—complete with a dotted line for the parent to detach, fill in, and return.

The **Student Record Profile Chart** is a guide for understanding and helping students, and offers a means of periodic evaluation. The chart is easy to use and provides all you need for accurate record keeping and measuring accountability for individual student progress throughout all seven units. It provides an accumulative skills profile for the student and represents an actual score of his or her written performance for each activity. Here is a workable form that you can immediately tailor to your own requirements for interpretation and use of scores. Included are clear instructions, with an example, to help you record your students' assessment on a day-to-day basis, to keep track of pupil progress, and to check learning patterns over a period of time. This chart allows you to spot the potential superior achiever along with the remedial individual. The chart coordinates all aspects of data ranging from the students' name, class, school, classroom teacher's name, semester, date, page number, actual grade, and attendance.

The **Word List** is presented as a reinforcement for building a music vocabulary. It emphasizes the use of dictionary skills; the students make a glossary of important words related to the particular unit. Its purpose is to encourage the use of vocabulary skills by helping develop an understanding of the music terms, concepts, and names found on the activity sheets. This vocabulary reference page is meant to be reproduced and used by the individual student throughout the units as a guide for spelling, word recognition, pronunciation, recording definitions, plus any other valuable information. Throughout six units of the *Library*, a cumulation of the words are presented on the Word List pages. (A Word List is not included in Unit 6.) With the help of this extensive vocabulary, when the student uses the words on both the activity page and the Word List, they will become embedded as part of his or her language.

Each Unit contains a wide-ranging collection of **Incentive Badges**. Use them to reward excellence, commend effort, for bonuses, prizes, behavior modification, or as reminders. These badges are designed to capture the interest and attention of the entire school. Several badges are designed with an open-ended format to provide maximum flexibility in meeting any special music teaching requirement.

Included in each Unit is a simple **Craft Project** that may be created by the entire class or by individual students. Each craft project is an integral part of the subject matter of that particular unit and will add a rich dimension to the activities. The materials necessary for the construction of the craft projects have been limited to those readily available in most classrooms and call for no special technical or artistic skills.

PLUS each Unit contains:

- Worked-out sample problems for students to use as a standard and model for their own work.

- Additional teaching suggestions in the Answer Key for getting the most out of certain activities.

- Extra staff paper for unlimited use, such as composing, ear training, improvising, or writing chords.

- Activities arranged in a sequential pattern.

Resources for Teaching Music More Effectively

- Have a classroom dictionary available for reference.
- Have a glossary or music dictionary available for reference.
- Use only one activity sheet per class session.
- Distribute the Word List prior to the first activity sheet of the particular unit. Encourage students to underline familiar words on the list and write definitions or identifications on the back before instruction on the unit begins. Later, the students can compare their answers with those studied.
- Provide short-term goals for each class session and inform students in advance that awards will be given for the day. You'll see how their conduct improves, too.
- Encourage students to make or buy an inexpensive folder to store music activity sheets, craft projects, word lists, self-evaluation charts, and so on. Folders might be kept in the classroom when not in use and distributed at the beginning of each class period.
- Many of the activities are ideal for bulletin board display. If space is not available to display all students' work, rotate the exhibits.
- Encourage students to re-read creative writing pages for clarity and accuracy before copying the final form on the activity sheet. Proofreading for grammatical and spelling errors should be encouraged.
- For creative drawing activities, encourage students to sketch their initial ideas on another sheet of paper first, then draw the finished product on the activity sheet. It is not necessary to have any technical ability in drawing to experience the pleasure of these creative activities.
- Although you will probably want to work through parts of some activities with your students, and choose some activities for group projects, you will find that most lessons are designed to lead students to the correct answers with little or no teacher direction. Students can be directed occasionally to work through an activity with a partner to search out and correct specific errors.
- Self-corrections and self-checking make a much better impression on young learners than do red-penciled corrections by the classroom music teacher.
- On activities where answers will vary, encourage students to rate their own work on correctness, originality, completeness, carefulness, realism, and organization.

• Most activity pages will serve as a "teacher assistant" in developing specific skills or subject areas to study. The activities throughout the series are complete with learning objectives and are generally factual enough for the teacher to use as a basis for a daily lesson plan.

• The library research activities promote creativity instead of copying while students search out relevant data from a variety of sources, such as encyclopedias, dictionaries, reference books, autobiographies, and others. These activities are ideal for the individual student or groups of students working beyond the classroom environment.

• The following are practical guidelines in planning, organizing, and constructing the Craft Projects:

. . . Acquaint yourself with any of the techniques that are new to you before you ask your students to undertake the project.

. . . Decide on your project and assemble the materials before you begin.

. . . Make a sample model for experience.

. . . Use a flat surface for working.

. . . Be sure the paper is cut exactly to measurements and that folds are straight.

. . . Be available for consultation.

. . . Provide guidance on what the next logical step is to encourage all students to finish their projects.

. . . Use the finished craft projects as displays and points of interest for your school's open house.

• Many of the Incentive Badges found in each Unit are open-ended and can be made effective communication tools to meet your needs. Extra space is provided on these badges for additional written messages that might be used for any number of reasons. Be creative for your own special needs; load the copier with colored paper and print as many as you need for the semester or entire school year. Then simply use a paper cutter to separate the badges and sort them out alphabetically. Make an alphabetical index on file card dividers using these titles. Next, arrange them in an accessible file box or shoe box, depending on the size needed. Include a roll of tape to attach the badge to the recipient.

Teacher's Guide to Unit 6

Special Days Throughout the Year is a rich resource for anyone working with music students. The activities in Unit 6 are fun to do while they relate music to the calendar year. The 50 activity sheets encompass 42 American special days that occur throughout the school calendar year, including summer school. There are 8 additional activities specifically designed for those days when class schedules are upset because of extracurricular activities such as field trips, rehearsals, and field day. There is even an activity entitled "Rainy Day Puzzle" to use when buses may be late.

Unit 6 is divided into two sections. "Holidays" follows the calendar year, beginning with Labor Day in September, and ending with National Aviation Day in August. Each activity is designed to provide the student with enjoyment as he or she looks forward to that particular holiday. The only advice on how to present these activities is to let your class relax and have fun with these lessons. Take the opportunity to relate what the student is learning in music class to history, geography, literature, or whatever the holiday represents. Do not feel you have to use every activity in this unit. It is better to cover less material and teach it well.

The second section, "Special Events," is created for those days when nothing goes as usual. When time schedules are interrupted and when a number of students are excused from the classroom, it is extremely difficult to carry on as usual. The activities in this section are self-explanatory.

The Contents in this unit lists the title of the activity with the corresponding special day in order, according to the school calendar year. Lively illustrations convey the spirit of important celebrations while providing an excellent introduction to each music activity.

As music always plays an integral part in our holiday celebrations, these activity sheets are the perfect way to stimulate interest and discussion about music through holidays and other occasions. There are lessons for teaching music skills, creative writing, music history, interesting music facts about certain holidays, songs related to holidays, and songs about other special days. Many activities may also be used in conjunction with American history lessons. By relating music to special days, students will broaden their awareness of historical events and deepen their own enthusiasm for music.

Contents

Contents

Activity Number/Title		Holiday or Special Day	Date	Level of Difficulty
Special Events				
6–43	MUSIC TERM REBUS	Field Day	Will vary	Beginner
6–44	POMP AND CIRCUMSTANCE	Graduation Day	Will vary	Intermediate
6–45	CAN YOU PICTURE THAT?	Last Day of School	Will vary	Beginner
6–46	THANK-YOU GRAM	After a Field Trip	Will vary	Beginner
6–47	BEGIN HERE	Rehearsal Day	Will vary	Beginner
6–48	RAINY DAY PUZZLE	Rainy Day	Will vary	Intermediate
6–49	FLASH BULLETIN	Musical Presentation	Will vary	Beginner
6–50	DESIGNING CONTEST	Musical Event	Will vary	Beginner

Activities for
HOLIDAYS

FULL STEAM AHEAD   6–1

Repair all the tracks leading to the roundhouse for this locomotive by placing four-letter words into each track. Use only the seven letter names of the notes below to form your four-letter words. Use each word only once. Letters may be used more than once in each word.

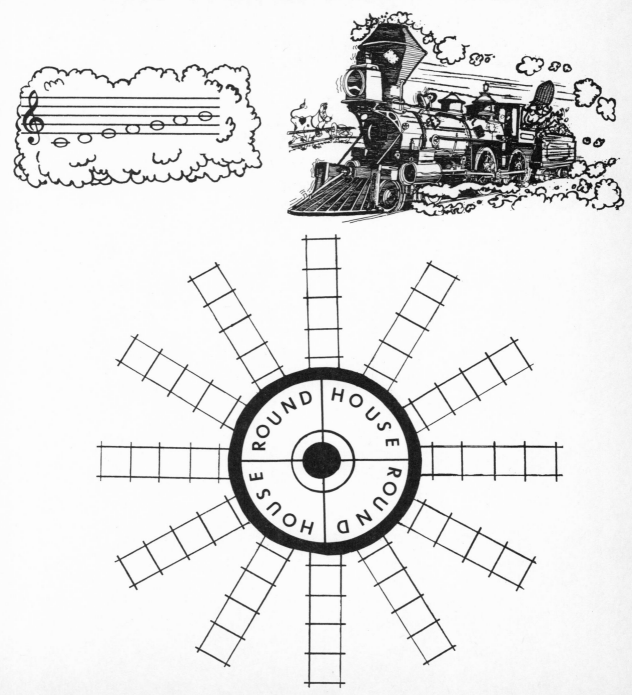

A NOTE OF THANKS   6–2

Write a letter to someone in the field of music who has inspired you. Make it a letter of appreciation to that person who has encouraged you to take private music lessons, who inspired you to attend a particular musical event, or who motivated you to do something musical. You decide the reason. Be sure your letter gets delivered when you're finished!

Name _____   Score _____

Date _____   Class _____

SOUNDING WORD-RHYTHMS

6–3

Discover the rhythms of these Indian names by tapping, clapping, and saying the words. Record the sounds of the words with notation using $\frac{2}{4}$ meter. An example is done for you. Some names may have more than one correct rhythm pattern.

INDIAN TRIBES

Cherokee $(\frac{2}{4})$ ♫ ♩ _____

1. Chocktaw _____

2. Hopi-Pueblo _____

3. Crow _____

4. Sioux _____

5. Seminole _____

CHIEFS AND LEADERS

6. Pontiac _____

7. Pocahontas _____

8. Sitting Bull _____

9. Squanto _____

RIVERS, TOWNS, CITIES, STATES

10. Mississippi _____

11. Flambeau _____

12. Arizona _____

13. Iowa _____

14. Miami _____

15. Chippewa _____

Name _____   Score _____

Date _____   Class _____

A TIME OF DISCOVERY

6–4

Each of these songs is appropriate to listen to on a special day of the year. Match the day with the song title by drawing connecting lines.

1. Handel's *Messiah*

2. "When Irish Eyes Are Smiling" by Ernest Ball

3. "We Shall Overcome"

4. "Sailing, Sailing"

5. "Song of Democracy" by Howard Hanson

6. "God of Our Fathers" National Hymn

7. "We Gather Together" folk song from the Netherlands

8. "A Paper of Pins" American Song

a. Thanksgiving

b. Valentine's Day

c. Martin Luther King's Birthday

d. Christmas

e. Columbus' Birthday

f. Memorial Day

g. Independence Day

h. St. Patrick's Day

ENTER THE CONTEST   6–5

A contest you have just heard about asks you to write a poem, or a verse, that could be set to music. Use these guidelines for your writing.

- Become acquainted with some fine poetry.
- Choose a happy subject matter for your poem.
- The end sound of each line should rhyme with the end sound in the following line or the line thereafter.
- Each line should stand alone.
- Each line should be a sentence.
- The words should be simple and easy to communicate.
- Avoid trite words and clichés.
- Make your poem original!

_____

_____

_____

_____

_____

_____

_____

_____

_____

_____

_____

_____

_____

_____

_____

_____

BE A LINGUIST   6–6

The following music words have been borrowed or adapted from other languages. Use your dictionary and write the country from which each word originates.

1. Alto _____

2. Aria _____

3. Ballet _____

4. Bass _____

5. Cadenza _____

6. Clef _____

7. Duet _____

8. Ensemble _____

9. Finale _____

10. Fine _____

11. Flute _____

12. Glissando _____

13. Glockenspiel _____

14. Horn _____

15. Impromptu _____

16. Klavier _____

17. Largo _____

18. Mazurka _____

19. Minuet _____

20. Nocturne _____

21. Noel _____

22. Oboe _____

23. Ostinato _____

24. Piano _____

25. Sonata _____

26. Timpani _____

27. Waltz _____

28. Zither _____

© 1987 by Parker Publishing Company, Inc.

Name _____   Score _____

Date _____   Class _____

GIVE US A CALL   6–7

Imagine that you work as a composer for a company that provides its customers with cassette tapes of singing telephone messages. You are in charge of figuring out the melody and writing the lyrics. For this tape you decide what the customer ordered. Some possibilities are: a special birthday, straight A's, holiday, or even a message for a telephone answering machine.

✳✳✳✳✳✳✳✳✳✳✳✳✳✳✳✳✳✳✳✳✳✳

Name of Customer: _____

Type of Tape Requested: _____

CELEBRATE WITH THE CLASSICS

What music would be appropriate to listen to on these special days? Draw an arrow from the special day to the music.

Halloween

Easter

Graduation Day

Wedding

1. *The Nutcracker* Suite by Peter Ilich Tchaikovsky

2. *Danse Macabre* by Camille Saint-Saëns

3. *A Lincoln Portrait* for narrator and orchestra by Aaron Copland

4. *Washington Post March* by John Philip Sousa

5. "Bridal March" from *Lohengrin* by Richard Wagner

6. *Stars and Stripes Forever* by John Philip Sousa

7. *Pomp and Circumstance* by Edward Elgar

8. The *Requiem* Mass by Giuseppe Verdi

Lincoln's Birthday

Flag Day

Christmas

Washington's Birthday

Name _____   Score _____

Date _____   Class _____

TAKE A PERSONAL OPINION POLL   6–9

Here is a list of statements that deal with music in one way or another. Read the list to ten individual students in your school. Record each person's opinion about the statements. Mark either AGREE, DISAGREE, or NO OPINION, by drawing a check mark (✔) opposite the statement and directly under the choice. (Do not record answers from a person who has already responded to the poll.) On the back of this page, number the paper from 1–10 and record the name of each person you polled.

STATEMENT	AGREE	DISAGREE	NO OPINION
1. A music class should be required for all students in our school.			
2. Every child should learn to play a musical instrument.			
3. Taking private music lessons is a privilege.			
4. We have adequate music facilities and instruments in our school.			
5. Every student in school should be allowed to attend at least two music field trips a year.			
6. Every person can learn to sing in tune.			
7. There should be more emphasis put on music in our school.			
8. Listening to classical music will make a person smarter.			
9. Left-handed people are more musically talented than right-handed people.			
10. There should be more classical music played by the radio stations.			

COPY CAT

6–10

Two of the staffs below are missing the notes. First sing through the melody. Then decide which phrase(s) in the song are repeated. Draw the notes on the staffs to complete the melody. Be sure to line the notes up with the words.

The Marines' Hymn

From the halls of Mon - te - zu - ma to the shores of Trip-o - li,_____

We will fight our coun-try's bat - tles on the land and on the sea._____

First to fight for right and free - dom, And to keep our hon-or clean,_____

We are proud to claim the ti - tle of U - nit - ed States Ma - rines!

Name _____   Score _____

Date _____   Class _____

I'M THANKFUL FOR . . .   6-11

Think of a simple familiar melody that you could
use to write new lyrics. The title of your new song
will be "I'm Thankful for . . ." Choose words that
you can easily communicate; ones that are simple
and easily sung. Remember, the important words of
the poem should fall on the accented beats of the
measures.

I'm Thankful for . . .

To the tune of: _____

RULES TO REMEMBER   6-12

Pretend that you have been asked to brief a new student on what has been happening in music class since the semester began. You are specifically asked to inform this student about certain rules to remember in music class. What are the rules? List them below.

Name _____   Score _____

Date _____   Class _____

WRITE THE LYRICS   6-13

Here is a familiar patriotic song. See how many of the words you know by memory. Write the lyrics to the song under the staffs. Be sure to match each syllable and word directly under the correct note.

CHRISTMAS STEP PUZZLES   6–14

Listed below are two puzzles with six Christmas song titles in each. All the song titles have one missing word. Write the missing word going across for numbers 1 through 5. Then, check your answers by reading #6 down. Those answers will complete the last titles.

A

1. "The _____ Noel"
2. "Silent _____"
3. "Joy to the _____"
4. "Jingle _____"
5. "Thirty-two Feet and _____ Little Tails"
6. "I Saw _____ Ships"

B

1. "Silver _____"
2. "It Came Upon the Midnight _____"
3. *The Nutcracker* _____
4. "Let It _____! Let It Snow! Let It Snow!"
5. "We _____ Kings of Orient Are"
6. "Jolly Old _____ Nicholas"

Name _____   Score _____

Date _____   Class _____

REARRANGE AULD LANG SYNE

6–15

The lines of this song were printed in the wrong order. Rewrite the
song on the staffs at the bottom in the correct order. Then carefully
print the words underneath the staffs.

Auld Lang Syne

A. auld____lang____syne, my dear, For   auld ____ lang ____ syne,   We'll

B. Should auld ac-quain-tance be for-got, And nev- er brought to mind? Should

C. tak'   a cup   o' kind-ness yet, For____ auld____ lang ____ syne.

D. auld   ac-quain-tance be for-got, And days of auld lang syne?   For

WHO'S WHO?   6–16

How many of these famous Black American musicians and singers do you know? A short description of each person is given below. Match the description to the name by writing the letter on the blank. Then check your answers with the answer key given at the bottom of the sheet.

_____ 1. MARIAN ANDERSON

_____ 2. LOUIS ARMSTRONG

_____ 3. DUKE ELLINGTON

_____ 4. MICHAEL JACKSON

_____ 5. EVA JESSYE

_____ 6. SCOTT JOPLIN

_____ 7. JELLY ROLL MORTON

_____ 8. LEONTYNE PRICE

_____ 9. GEORGE SHIRLEY

a. Known as the "King of Ragtime"; wrote "The Maple Leaf Rag"

b. Was selected by Gershwin to be choral director for his first production of "Porgy and Bess"

c. Was regarded as the first true jazz composer

d. Became the world's leading contralto singer of the 20th century

e. Said "Good music is music that sounds good"; by 1970, had written more than 2,000 compositions

f. Was one of the leading prima donnas of the opera in the 1950s and 1960s with the "voice of the century"

g. Was the leading male singer of the Metropolitan Black Opera in the 1960s

h. A sensational singer of the 1980s with record sales in the millions

i. Was the first great jazz soloist; was one of jazz's most creative innovators not only with the trumpet, but with his style of singing, too

© 1987 by Parker Publishing Company, Inc.

ANSWER KEY: d, i, e, h, b, a, c, f, g

© 1987 by Parker Publishing Company, Inc.

Name _____   Score _____

Date _____   Class _____

PATRIOTIC PARADE

Listed below are the beginning lines of ten patriotic songs. Each is missing the next word. Find the word in the puzzle by reading across, downward, or diagonally. Then write the missing word on the blank to finish the first line of the song.

1. Oh, beautiful for spacious

   _____

2. Mine eyes have seen the

   _____

3. Over hill, over

   _____

4. Columbia, the gem of the

   _____

5. I'm a Yankee Doodle

   _____

6. From the halls of

   _____

7. Oh, say can you see,
   by the dawn's early

   _____

8. Father and I went down to

   _____

9. You're a grand old flag,
   you're a high flying

   _____

10. God bless America, land that I

    _____

C	L	D	A	N	D	Y	O	A	Z
S	K	I	E	S	M	G	B	U	E
A	G	X	G	B	O	M	T	M	G
T	L	E	F	H	N	G	I	T	J
R	O	I	Z	Q	T	T	L	M	C
B	R	D	A	L	E	F	H	O	O
F	Y	M	L	B	Z	C	P	C	L
R	L	E	R	T	U	U	I	E	O
W	E	A	C	A	M	P	M	A	V
B	V	D	G	X	A	I	O	N	E

Color in the star if you can list the names of the songs from 1 to 10 on the back of this page.

HAIL TO THE CHIEF   6–18

Imagine that you have been asked to write a tribute to the President. Use the clef of your instrument and compose a song below. Words are optional.

Name _____   Score _____

Date _____   Class _____

MAKE A TOUCHDOWN

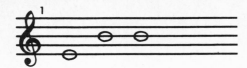

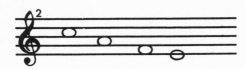

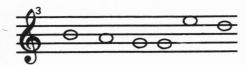

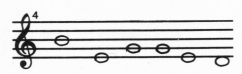

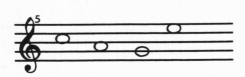

Each of the sets of notes below spells a word. Write your answers on the football to discover a seven-letter word reading across the diamond area.

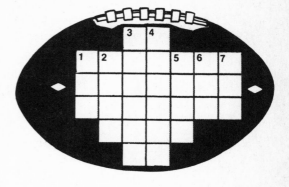

Make a touchdown by writing the seven-letter word here.

___ ___ ___ ___ ___ ___ ___

WHAT DO YOU SEE?   6–20

This balloon everyone is smiling at is promoting music at your school. It might have a slogan, some type of message, or even a musical design. You decide what it is and carefully draw your idea.

Name _____   Score _____

Date _____   Class _____

LINCOLN'S DAYDREAM   6–21

In his time, Abe Lincoln probably did his share of daydreaming. Imagine that he was thinking about playing a musical instrument. Draw his dream.

SEND A LOVE-GRAM   6–22

Send a personalized valentine this year to someone special. First write the lyrics and compose a song by writing the words in syllables and matching up each note directly above. Then, copy your song on the LOVE-GRAM below and color the valentines.

Name _____   Score _____

Date _____   Class _____

I CANNOT TELL A LIE

Here are some statements about the music during the time of George Washington. "Tell the truth" by circling the correct ending for each statement.

1. During the American Revolution, children sang songs like "Here We Go 'Round the Mulberry Bush" and "London Bridge" . . .

   a. in the classroom.   b. along with the radio.
   c. while playing singing games.

2. The first songs sung in the Colonies were traditional songs brought from . . .

   a. Africa.   b. Britain.   c. Italy.

3. Most singing during the early Colonial days was . . .

   a. unaccompanied.   b. jazz-like.   c. barbershop style.

4. Early settlers generally sang traditional songs by memory, passing them on by . . .

   a. hand.   b. pigeon.   c. word of mouth.

5. The ballads of the American Revolution were almost like "singing newspapers" because they were . . .

   a. delivered daily.   b. written on newsprint.
   c. in verse form, giving news of the battles.

6. An important role in the printing and distribution of new ballads was . . .

   a. electricity.   b. the printing press.   c. the cotton gin.

7. In the mountains of Kentucky and Tennessee, a popular instrument was the . . .

   a. recorder.   b. xylophone.   c. dulcimer.

8. The instruments that accompanied the colonials as they marched off to war were the . . .

   a. fife and drum.   b. Marine Band.   c. bugle corps.

9. The fretless banjo was developed by . . .

   a. American Indians.   b. the first settlers.   c. Black slaves.

10. Music was so important to the Colonists because . . .

   a. it provided a common tradition.   b. they liked to square dance.
   c. it was the only thing they brought with them from the old country.

SKIP IT   6-24

There is a wrong note in each complete measure of this song. Cross out each of these extra notes. The first one is done for you. The rewrite "Happy Birthday" on the staffs below, skipping the notes that you crossed out. Write the verse from memory underneath the staffs. Be sure to line up each syllable and word with the correct note.

Happy Birthday

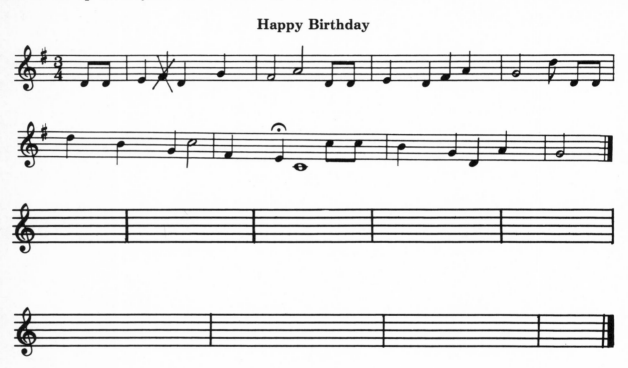

Name _____   Score _____

Date _____   Class _____

WE'RE #1   6–25

All these parents pictured think your school will be the number one school in the country for promoting "Music in our Schools Month." Make a list of all the ways your school *should* promote music during the month of March. (Consider concerts, public speakers, poster contests, field trips, essays, and a talent show for a start!) Be specific, original, and tell how you'll participate in at least one of your suggested ideas. If you need extra space, use the back of this page.

_____

_____

_____

_____

_____

_____

_____

_____

_____

_____

_____

_____

_____

_____

_____

_____

Name _____ Score _____

Date _____ Class _____

SHAMROCK PUZZLE   6–26

Listed below are five song titles. Each has a missing word. Write the missing word across the matching blocks of the puzzle. Then the sixth word, which reads down, will spell a musical term. Write the term in the blank by its definition.

1. "God _____ America"

2. "_____ of the Sugarplum Fairy"

3. "He's Got the _____ World in His Hands"

4. "My Wild _____ Rose"

5. "_____ Night When the Sun Goes Down

6. _____:
   Includes all the parts for the different instruments and voices needed in a piece of music; written one above the other on a single page.

WHAT'S IN COMMON?   6-27

Each of the following groups of words has something in common. Find the answer from the words on the bottom and write the answer in the blank.

_____   1. Rumba, boogie, polka, mazurka, waltz, fox trot, tango, polonaise, bop, swing

_____   2. "Here Comes Peter Cottontail," "The Easter Parade," "Bunny Boogie"

_____   3. Chorale, plainsong, mass, motet, church cantata, anthem

_____   4. p, mp, pp, f, ff, mf

_____   5. Whole, half, quarter, eighth, sixteenth

_____   6. French horn, trumpet, cornet, trombone, tuba

_____   7. Kettledrums, xylophone, chimes, tambourine, triangle, cymbals, bass drum, maracas

_____   8. Clarinet, oboe, saxophone, English horn, bass clarinet, bassoon, flute, piccolo

_____   9. Violin, viola, cello, double bass, harp

_____   10. Piano, organ, harpsichord, clavichord, synthesizer

_____   11. Handel, Bach, Vivaldi, Mozart, Beethoven

_____   12. Hot cross buns, hard-boiled eggs, new clothes, Easter rabbit, roast lamb, sunrise services

woodwinds / keyboard / dynamic markings
popular Easter songs / religious music
strings / brass / dances / composers
notes / percussion / Easter traditions

WHAT HAPPENED THEN?   6-28

Using the note clues, fill in the missing words on the blanks. Then write an ending to this silly rhyming story. Use at least four new "note words" in your conclusion. Use the back of this paper if you need more space.

A girl named _____ sat

in a _____ with a _____

in a _____ .

FINISH THE TITLE   6–29

These song titles, having to do with trees or shrubs of one kind or another, are all missing one word. The missing word can be found in the puzzle. Write the matching number in the block and write the answer on the blanks. The first one is done for you.

a. [9] "Autumn L E A V E S

b. [ ] "Green ___ ___ ___ ___
        the Rushes-Oh"

c. [ ] "Over the River and Through the
        ___ ___ ___ ___"

d. [ ] "I Gave My Love
        A ___ ___ ___ ___ ___ ___"
        (The Riddle)

e. [ ] "In the Shade of the Old
        ___ ___ ___ ___ Tree"

f. [ ] "___ ___ ___ ___ ___ ___ ___ ___"

g. [ ] "Hickory Dickory ___ ___ ___ ___"

h. [ ] "___ ___ ___ ___ ___ ___ ___ ___ ___ ___"
        (Sits on the Old Gum Tree)

i. [ ] "I Had a Little ___ ___ ___ Tree"

j. [ ] "Here We Go 'Round the Mulberry ___ ___ ___ ___"

k. [ ] "The ___ ___ ___ ___   ___ ___ ___ ___ ___"

l. [ ] "Oranges and ___ ___ ___ ___ ___ ___"

m. [ ] "Tie a Yellow Ribbon 'Round the Old ___ ___ ___ Tree"

n. [ ] "There Was a Tree Stood in the ___ ___ ___ ___ ___ ___"

o. [ ] "Under the Spreading ___ ___ ___ ___ ___ ___ ___ ___ Tree"

Crossword puzzle answers:
1. POINCIANA
2. NUT
3. ASHGROVE
4. WOODS
5. DOCK
6. KOOKABARRA
7. GROW
8. CHERRY
9. LEAVES
10. APPLE
11. BUSH
12. GROUND
13. CHESTNUT
14. OAK
(also LEMON)

Name _____   Score _____

Date _____   Class _____

COMPOSER WORD SEARCH   6–30

It was known that Thomas Jefferson (1743–1826) was gifted with a fine voice. Not only did he enjoy singing, but he often played violin duets with Patrick Henry (1736–1799). Music performed during Jefferson's time was written by some of his contemporaries like Mozart (1756–1791) and Haydn (1732–1809). Their music was influenced by many of the composers listed below. Notice that some letters are missing in all the composers' last names. Figure out the spelling of these composers' names by circling them in the word search. The names can be found reading across and down. Write the missing letters of the last names on the blanks.

```
N A Z U B J
O E N B E W Y B
P X A E M Y W U
I Y M O Y W M X
Z O S E P Y L O T
I Y W L I M B N E
P U R C E L L Y T H
Q I C Q M T J S I E U
E R D Z Y M B B A C H C M V D
C M M D A C Y Y Z M E A A E E
O X I M M O R L E Y Y R I R P
R O C L A R D U D M O L P D Q
E T M P X Y W J L M E A C I Y
L E F I D K L M O W T T W Y Z
L V I V A L D I M O S T U C X
I M E W Y O I M W Y C I Y O P
```

1. JOHANN SEBASTIAN B _ _ H
   (1685–1750)

2. DIETRICH B _ _ _ _ _ _ _ E
   (1637–1707)

3. WILLIAM B _ _ D
   (1543–1623)

4. ARCANGELO C _ _ _ _ _ _ I
   (1653–1713)

5. CLAUDIO M _ _ _ _ _ _ _ _ I
   (1567–1643)

6. THOMAS M _ _ _ _ _ Y
   (1557–1602)

7. HENRY P _ _ _ _ _ _ L
   (1659–1695)

8. ALESSANDRO and DOMENICO
   S _ _ _ _ _ _ _ I
   (1660–1725)   (1683–1757)

9. GEORGE T _ _ _ _ _ _ _ N
   (1681–1761)

10. ANTONIO V _ _ _ _ _ _ I
    (1676–1741)

HOW DOES IT LOOK?   6–31

Match these names with the right Latin American instruments by writing the correct letter after the name. Check your answers with the list at the bottom. Then draw the right instrument in each box.

1. Claves ___	2. Cowbell ___	3. Guiro ___	4. Guitar ___
5. Maracas ___	6. Marimba ___	7. Timbales ___	8. Steel Drums ___

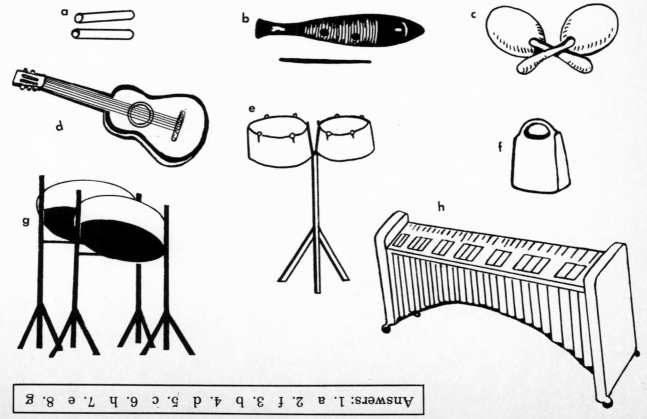

Answers: 1. a 2. f 3. b 4. d 5. c 6. h 7. e 8. g

Name _____   Score _____

Date _____   Class _____

YANKEE DOODLE   6–32

The song "Yankee Doodle" developed into the most important song of the American Revolution. The measures below from the verse of the song are all mixed up. Sing through the first verse to decide where each measure should be placed, and write that measure's letter in the appropriate place. The first measure is done for you.

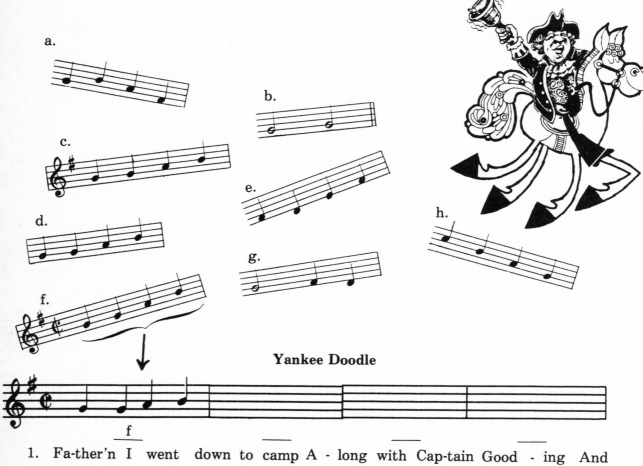

Yankee Doodle

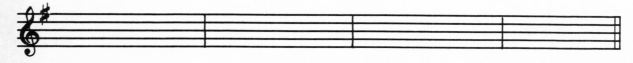

1. Fa-ther'n I went down to camp A - long with Cap-tain Good - ing And

there we saw the men and boys As thick as hast - y pud - ding

SOLVE THE REBUS PUZZLES   6–33

Follow the signs to add or subtract the letters in the names of the objects to solve the puzzles.
The blanks after the equals signs tell how many letters the answer contains. Check your answer
with the clue at the left. Each answer is the name of a song.

The southern states of America as a group are sometimes given this name.	**1** — she + ▸ — sa + ⚁ — dc = _ _ _ _ _
A popular water sport especially on lakes.	**2** s + ∫ — t + ○ — r = _ _ _ _ _ _ _
In a child's imagination this is a wonderful place.	**3** — ca + ▸ — b + ▸ — ion + ✋ — h = _ _ _ _ _ _ _
A patriotic song written by Samuel F. Smith.	**4** — lp + ♡ — 🎩 + — me + a = _ _ _ _ _ _ _

Present your mom with a personalized Mother's Day card this year. Below is the melody to "If
You're Happy." Write your own lyrics, making the words appropriate for Mother's Day. You
may tie (♫) notes together to make the words fit the melody line. Carefully write the words
directly under the staffs to match the notes. Give your song a title and write it in the middle
above the first staff. Write your name after "words by." When you're finished, color the picture.

DE COLORES (ALL IN COLOR) 6-34

The song titles and lyrics below have missing words that are names of colors. Choose from the following colors to complete the missing words:

red, yellow, blue, white, gray, black, brown, green

1. "_____ sleeves"   _____ sleeves was all my joy,

   _____ sleeves was my delight.

   _____ sleeves was my heart of gold,

   And who but my Lady _____ sleeves.

2. "Little _____ Jug"   Ha! Ha! Ha! you and me, little

   _____ jug don't I love thee!

3. "_____ River Valley"   But remember the _____ River Valley
   And the girl that has loved you so true.

4. "The _____ Tail Fly"   He died and the jury wondered why—

   The verdict was the _____ tail fly.

5. "The _____ Rose of Texas"   There's a _____ rose of Texas
   That I am going to see,
   No other fellow knows her, no fellow,
   only me;

6. "Old _____ Joe"   I'm coming, I'm coming,
   For my head is bending low;
   I hear those gentle voices calling,

   "Old _____ Joe!"

7. "The _____,   Thy banners make tyranny tremble,

   _____, and   When borne by the _____,

   _____"   _____ and _____.

REWRITE THE VERSE 6-36

The instrumental version of the song "Taps" is familiar to most people. The words to this song are included here. Rewrite the first verse of the song under the staffs. Be careful to place each word and syllable under the correct note.

Taps

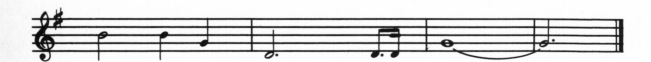

1. Fading light dims the sight
   And a star gems the sky,
      gleaming bright.
   From afar drawing nigh
   Falls the night.

2. Day is done, gone the sun
   From the lake, from the hills,
      from the sky
   All is well, safely rest;
   God is nigh.

3. Then good night, peaceful night,
   Till the light of the dawn
      shineth bright;
   God is near, do not fear
   Friend, good night.

TEST ON TAPS   6–37

A melody can be composed from as few as three or four notes. The composer may repeat the notes or arrange them in different ways. Study the song, "Taps," below to complete the following.

1. Finish numbering the measures of the song on top of the staffs. The first complete measure is numbered for you.

2. Write the letter names of the notes on the blanks under the staffs.

3. Write the letter names of the notes used in the song on this line:

   _____

4. Circle three more sets of repeated notes like the circled example. (The note lengths may vary.)

5. Draw a block around the pair of repeated notes that look just like the first two notes in the song.

Taps

Solemnly

WHAT COMES NEXT?   6-38

Here are the beginning lyrics to popular patriotic songs. Finish the line by writing the correct word on the blank. Choose your answer from the list below.

1. "Yankee Doodle went to _____."

2. "I'm a Yankee Doodle _____."

3. "You're a grand old _____."

4. "Oh, beautiful for spacious _____."

5. "God bless America, land that I _____."

6. "Oh, say can you see by the dawn's early _____."

7. "This land is your _____."

8. "Mine eyes have seen the glory of the coming of the _____."

9. "My country 'tis of _____."

10. "Over hill, over dale, as we hit the dusty _____."

11. "From the halls of Montezuma to the shores of _____."

12. "When Johnny comes marching home again, _____."

13. "The eyes of Texas are upon _____."

14. "Hail Columbia, happy _____."

15. "Columbia, the gem of the _____."

love
Thee
you
land
town
light
Lord
trail
Tripoli
dandy
land
skies
ocean
hurrah
flag

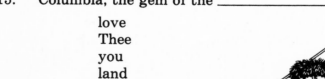

A SINGING TELEGRAM   6–39

For Father's Day this year, send a personalized message to that someone special. Here's the melody of the song, "For He's a Jolly Good Fellow." First decide who will receive the message. Then write your own lyrics, being careful to match the notes with your words under each staff. Be sure your message gets delivered on Father's Day. You could ask a friend to sing your greeting over the phone or in person; or you could sing the message yourself.

To the tune of: For He's a Jolly Good Fellow

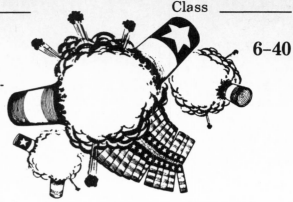

DOT THE BATTLE HYMN

6-40

Finish "The Battle Hymn of the Republic" by adding the dots for all *29* dotted notes.

Battle Hymn of the Republic

Words by Julia Ward Howe

Mine eyes have seen the glo - ry of the com - ing of the Lord;

He is tram - pling out the vin - tage where the grapes of wrath are stored;

He has loosed the fate - ful light - ning of His ter - ri - ble swift sword;

His truth is march - ing on.

Glo - ry, Glo - ry, Hal - le - lu - jah! Glo - ry, Glo - ry, Hal - le - lu - jah!

Glo - ry, Glo - ry, Hal - le - lu - jah! His truth is march - ing on.

Name _____   Score _____

Date _____   Class _____

PRESENT YOUR PICTURE   6–41

Draw a picture of your band or choir director, or your music teacher on the job. Then, as a great master would, sign your portrait in the bottom right-hand corner. When you are finished, cut along the dotted line and present your picture to the appropriate person.

OUT OF THIS WORLD   6–42

Over the years, composers and lyricists have often used the names of heavenly bodies in their song titles. Unscramble the words below, in the order as they appear, to discover the names of these songs.

When you are finished, think of other songs that use the words "star," "moon," or "sun" and write these titles on the back of this sheet.

1. REEH   MOCES   HET   NUS

   _____

2. OUY   REA   YM   UNSSINHE

   _____

3. TACCH   A   LAFLING   ATRS

   _____

4. NOMO   VORE   IMIMA

   _____

5. HWEN   OYU   SHWI   PUON   A   RATS

   _____

6. WINKLET   WINKLET   TILLTE   TARS

   _____

7. SINGINGW   NO   A   ARTS

   _____

8. SATRS   NAD   TRIPESS   ERERVOF

   _____

Activities for
SPECIAL EVENTS

© 1987 by Parker Publishing Company, Inc.

Name _____   Score _____

Date _____   Class _____

MUSIC TERM REBUS   6–43

Follow the signs to add or subtract the letters in the names of the objects to solve the puzzles. The blanks after the equals signs tell how many letters the answer contains. Check your answer with the clue at the left. Each answer is the name of a music term.

Tones of chords sung or played in succession.	1. (harp) + (potato) − h + (lion) − ln = _ _ _ _ _ _ _ _
A male voice between tenor and bass.	2. (barn) + (mitten) − nm + 1 − ten = _ _ _ _ _ _ _ _
There is one for the Meter and one for the Key.	3. (Garage Sale) + (cat) − c + (steeple) − ch ch + e = _ _ _ _ _ _ _ _ _
To upset the normal pulse of the meter, accent, and rhythm.	4. (star) − tar + (eye) − ee + n + (cow) − w + (bird) − rr + (hedgehog) − ol = _ _ _ _ _ _ _ _ _ _ _ _

POMP AND CIRCUMSTANCE

6–44

ACROSS

1. Stately display; splendor
2. *Pomp and Circumstance* was written in a _____ key.
3. The composer of this march was _____.
4. Sir Edward _____ was born in 1857.
5. Elgar's father was a _____ musician.

DOWN

6. Elgar's best-known orchestral music is the _____ Variations.
7. Elgar's _____ wanted him to become a lawyer.
8. Elgar played the _____.
9. *Pomp and Circumstance* is a world famous _____.
10. This piece is a _____ (*abbreviation*) graduation march.

CAN YOU PICTURE THAT?   6–45

You can make a picture of a double bass with these six puzzle pieces. Here are three suggestions of how to make your picture:

Trace the pieces and paste them on the puzzle.
            OR
Cut out the pieces and paste them on the puzzle.
            OR
Carefully draw what is shown into the corresponding pieces of the puzzle.

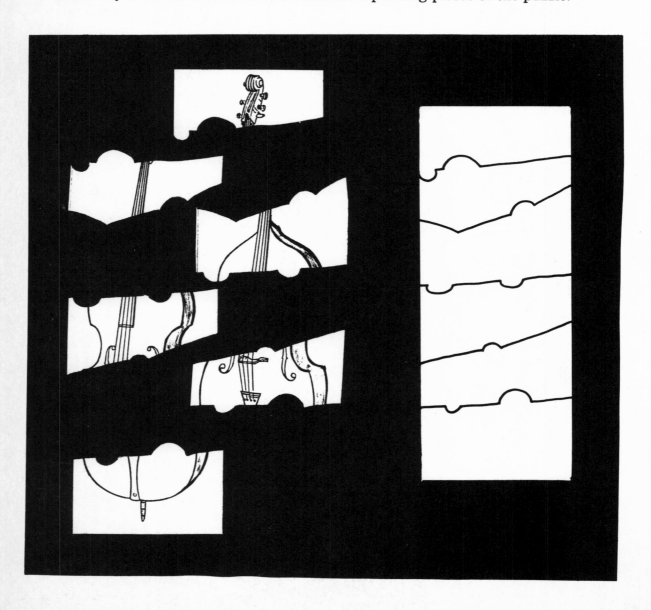

THANK-YOU GRAM   6–46

Write a note of thanks to someone who helped make a certain musical event or field trip possible. That special person could be a chaperone, the director, teacher, conductor, performer, or even the bus driver.

- ✂ - - -

THANK-YOU GRAM:

_____
_____
_____
_____
_____
_____
_____
_____
_____
_____
_____
_____

Name _____   Score _____

Date _____   Class _____

BEGIN HERE   6–47

Finish drawing those outlines of instruments played in military marching bands. Use the extra space below to name and draw other instruments used in this type of marching band.

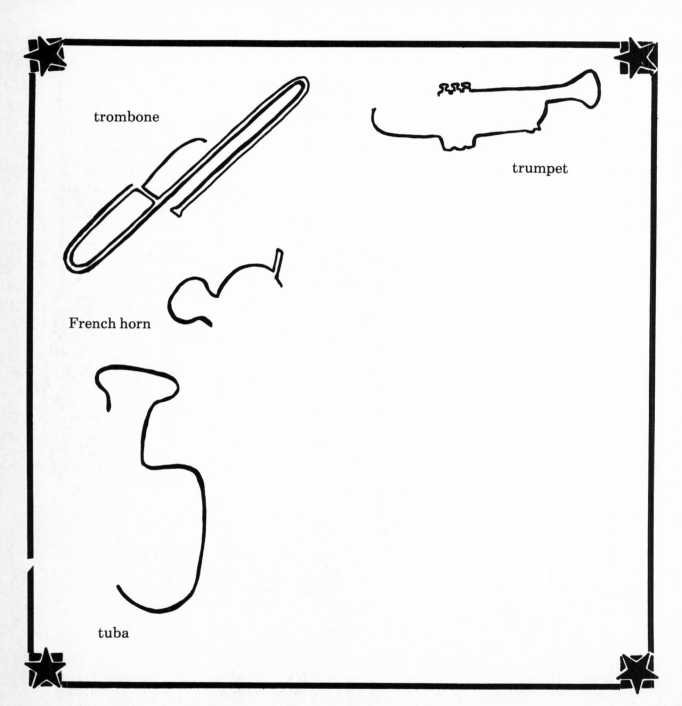

Name _____   Score _____

Date _____   Class _____

RAINY DAY PUZZLE   6–48

Have you ever gone 'round and 'round to get somewhere? In this puzzle that is what you will do. To reach the middle, fill in the blocks with the words suggested by the clues. The last letter of the first word is the first letter of the second word, and so on.

1. Tuba—a large _____.
2. A very quick Italian dance.
3. Extra sharp, flat or natural not already in the key signature
4. The words of an opera.
5. (It.) A short repeated melody.
6. Covers eight notes of any scale.
7. 𝄾 is an _____ rest.
8. ⌢ is a __ or pause sign
9. _____ after notes increase their length.
10. The seventh syllable of a Major scale; may also be written as "ti."

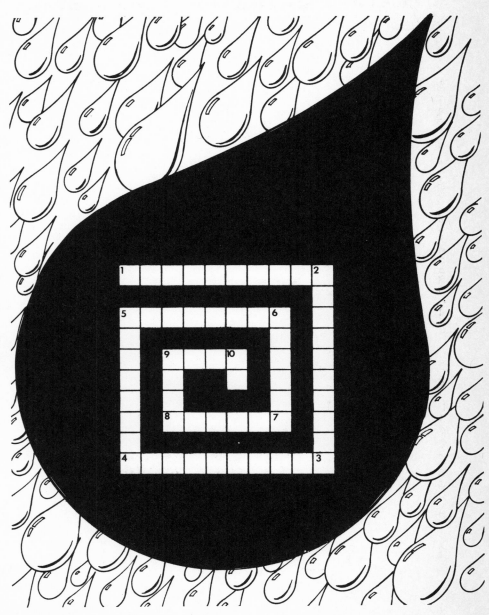

FLASH BULLETIN   6–49

Imagine that you are in charge of sending a bulletin home to students and parents notifying them of an upcoming event. Use the space below to tell about this special musical event coming to your school, and what type of a performance it will be. Mention the date, place, time, and price of admission. Tell about who's going to be in it and why someone would want to attend.

DESIGNING CONTEST   6–50

Use the space below to design a poster for a special musical event coming to your community or school. In your promotion, include the time, place, and date, along with who's performing. Use illustrations, different styles of lettering, and/or different colors to make it interesting. Remember, it has to be neat if you want people to read it!

Answer Key
for *Music for Special Days*

6-1 FULL STEAM AHEAD

Suggested answers include: abed, aged, bade, bead, beef, cafe, cage, dead, deaf, face, fade, feed, gage

6-2 A NOTE OF THANKS

Answers will vary.

6-3 SOUNDING WORD-RHYTHMS

Suggested answers are:

1. ♩♩
2. ♫♩
3. ♩
4. ♩
5. ♫♩
6. ♫♩
7. ♫♫
8. ♫♩

9. ♩♩
10. ♫♩
11. ♩♩
12. ♫♩
13. ♫♩
14. ♫♩
15. ♫♩

The names of some North American Indians are shown in picture language. They are Lazy Boy, Curly Bear, Berry Woman, and Wades-in-Water.

6-4 A TIME OF DISCOVERY

1. d
2. h
3. c
4. e

5. g
6. f
7. a
8. b

6-5 ENTER THE CONTEST

Answers will vary.

6-6 BE A LINGUIST

Students will need a dictionary for this activity. You might have students write the definitions of unfamiliar words on the back of the activity sheet.

1.	French/Italian	15.	French
2.	Italian	16.	German
3.	French	17.	Italian
4.	Italian/German	18.	Italian
5.	Italian	19.	French
6.	Latin	20.	French
7.	French	21.	French
8.	French	22.	Italian
9.	Italian	23.	Italian
10.	Italian	24.	Italian
11.	French	25.	Italian
12.	Italian	26.	Italian
13.	German	27.	German
14.	German	28.	German

6-7 GIVE US A CALL

Answers will vary.

6-8 CELEBRATE WITH THE CLASSICS

1.	Christmas	5.	Wedding
2.	Halloween	6.	Flag Day
3.	Lincoln's Birthday	7.	Graduation Day
4.	Washington's Birthday	8.	Easter

6-9 TAKE A PERSONAL OPINION POLL

Answers will vary.

6-10 COPY CAT

Review pick-up notes and incomplete measures with the students. Explain that the last two beats of the first measure are found in the final measure of the song. Lines 2 and 4 of the song are identical to the first line (staff) of the song.

6-11 I'M THANKFUL FOR . . .

Answers will vary.

6-12 RULES TO REMEMBER

Encourage the students to list rules in a positive way. For example, they can say "Raise your hand when you have the answer" instead of "Don't shout out the answer."

6-13 WRITE THE LYRICS

My coun - try, 'tis of thee, Sweet land of lib - er - ty, Of thee I sing. Land where my fa - thers died, Land of the pil - grims' pride, From ev - 'ry moun - tain - side, Let free-dom ring.

6-14 CHRISTMAS STEP PUZZLES

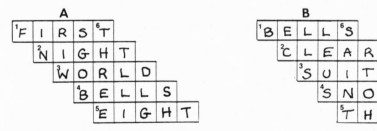

6-15 REARRANGE AULD LANG SYNE

The correct order is B, D, A, C.

6-16 WHO'S WHO?

This activity is self-checking. Encourage students to use this sheet as a study guide to become familiar with these famous Black American singers and musicians. Then play this simple game: Choose a leader. Ask the leader to read one description from the bottom of the page while the players have the activity sheet face down in front of them. The player who raises his or her hand first is called upon to identify the famous person. The leader must watch carefully for second or third hands in case the first player's answer is incorrect. The player who answers correctly is then the leader and continues the game.

6–17 PATRIOTIC PARADE

1. skies
2. glory
3. dale
4. ocean
5. dandy
6. Montezuma
7. light
8. camp
9. flag
10. love

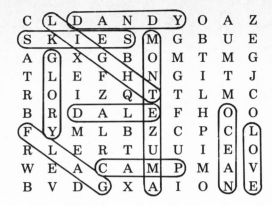

6–18 HAIL TO THE CHIEF

Answers will vary.

6–19 MAKE A TOUCHDOWN

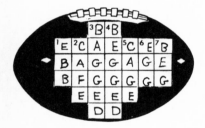

6–20 WHAT DO YOU SEE?

Answers will vary.

6–21 LINCOLN'S DAYDREAM

Answers will vary.

6–22 SEND A LOVE-GRAM

Answers will vary.

6–23 I CANNOT TELL A LIE

1. c
2. b
3. a
4. c
5. c

6. b
7. c
8. a
9. c
10. a

6–24 SKIP IT

Hap-py Birth-day to you, Hap-py Birth-day to you, Hap-py

Birth-day, dear _____, Hap-py Birth-day to you.

6–25 WE'RE #1

Answers will vary.

6–26 SHAMROCK PUZZLE

6–27 WHAT'S IN COMMON?

1. dances
2. popular Easter songs
3. religious music
4. dynamic markings
5. notes
6. brasses

7. percussion
8. woodwinds
9. strings
10. keyboard
11. composers
12. Easter traditions

6–28 WHAT HAPPENED THEN?

Beginner students may need to refer to the following guide while completing the activity. Copy this on the chalkboard:

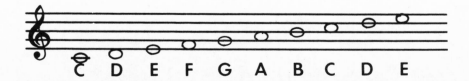

C D E F G A B C D E

Beginning answers are: A girl named *Bab* sat in a *cab* with a *gag* in a *bag*. The remaining answers will vary.

6–29 FINISH THE TITLE

a.   9 – Leaves

b.   7 – Grow

c.   4 – Woods

d.   8 – Cherry

e.   10 – Apple

f.   1 – Poinciana

g.   5 – Dock

h.   6 – Kookaburra

i.   2 – Nut

j.   11 – Bush

k.   3 – Ash Grove

l.   9 – Lemons

m. 14 – Oak

n.   12 – Ground

o.   13 – Chestnut

6–30 COMPOSER WORD SEARCH

1. BACH
2. BUXTEHUDE
3. BYRD
4. CORELLI
5. MONTEVERDI
6. MORLEY
7. PURCELL
8. SCARLATTI
9. TELEMANN
10. VIVALDI

```
          N A Z U B J
        O E N B E W Y B
        P X A E M Y W U
        I Y M O Y W M X
        Z O S E P Y L O T
        I Y W L I M B N E
        P U R C E L L Y T H
        Q I C Q M T J S I E U
    E R D Z Y M B B A C H C M V D
    C M M D A C Y Y Z M E A A E
    O X I M M O R L E Y Y R I R P
    R O C L A R D U D M O L P D Q
    E T M P X Y W J L M E A C U
    L E F I D K L M O W T T W Y Z
    L V I V A L D I M O S T U C X
    I M E W Y O I M W Y C I Y O P
```

6–31 HOW DOES IT LOOK?

This activity is self-checking.

6–32 YANKEE DOODLE

f, a, d, g, c, h, e, b

6–33 SOLVE THE REBUS PUZZLES

1. Dixie

2. Sailing

3. Toyland

4. America

6–34 DE COLORES (ALL IN COLOR)

1. Green

2. Brown

3. Red

4. Blue

5. Yellow

6. Black

7. Red, White, and Blue

8. Gray

6–35 MOM'S MUSICAL CARD

Answers will vary.

6-36 REWRITE THE VERSE

Fad-ing light   dims the sight   And   a   star gems the sky gleam-ing bright, From a-

far   draw - ing   nigh   Falls the night.

6-37 TEST ON TAPS

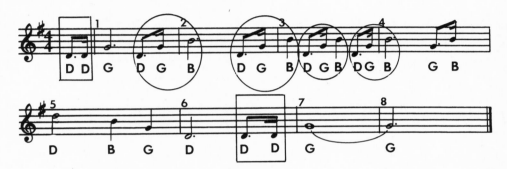

6-38 WHAT COMES NEXT?

1. town
2. dandy
3. flag
4. skies
5. love
6. light
7. land
8. Lord

9. Thee
10. trail
11. Tripoli
12. hurrah
13. you
14. land
15. ocean

6-39 A SINGING TELEGRAM

Play or sing the song "For He's a Jolly Good Fellow" to familiarize the students with the melody line.

6-40 DOT THE BATTLE HYMN

Play or sing the ''Battle Hymn of the Republic'' to familiarize the students with the rhythm.

6-41 PRESENT YOUR PICTURE

Answers will vary.

6-42 OUT OF THIS WORLD

1. HERE COMES THE SUN
2. YOU ARE MY SUNSHINE
3. CATCH A FALLING STAR
4. MOON OVER MIAMI
5. WHEN YOU WISH UPON A STAR
6. TWINKLE, TWINKLE LITTLE STAR
7. SWINGING ON A STAR
8. STARS AND STRIPES FOREVER

Other songs students might think of include:
OH MISTER MOON
YOU ARE THE SUNSHINE OF MY LIFE
SEASONS IN THE SUN
SUNSHINE ON MY SHOULDER
MOONLIGHT BAY
GOOD DAY SUNSHINE
STARDUST

6-43 MUSIC TERM REBUS

1. arpeggio
2. baritone
3. signature
4. syncopation

6–44 POMP AND CIRCUMSTANCE

For beginner students, you might supply the first letter of each word.

6–45 CAN YOU PICTURE THAT?

6–46 THANK-YOU GRAM

Answers will vary.

6–47 BEGIN HERE

Students' drawings will not be as detailed as these. Just be sure the illustrations show the general outlines.

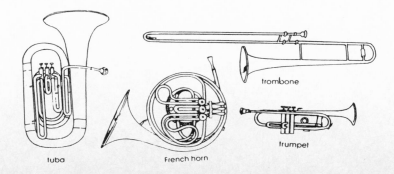

6–48 RAINY DAY PUZZLE

For beginner students, you might supply the first letter of each word.

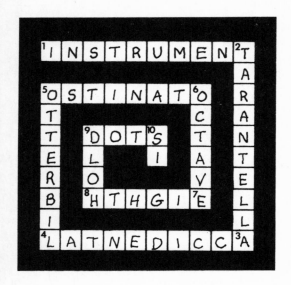

6–49 FLASH BULLETIN

Answers will vary.

6–50 DESIGNING CONTEST

Answers will vary.

Progress Chart
for *Special Days Throughout the Year*

Use this chart to keep a record of activities completed for each class. List your classes (or students) in the given spaces at the right. As each activity is completed for a class, mark an "X" in the appropriate column.

Activity Number/Title		Holiday or Special Day				
Holidays						
6–1	FULL STEAM AHEAD	Labor Day				
6–2	A NOTE OF THANKS	Citizenship Day				
6–3	SOUNDING WORD-RHYTHMS	American Indian Day				
6–4	A TIME OF DISCOVERY	Columbus Day				
6–5	ENTER THE CONTEST	Poetry Day				
6–6	BE A LINGUIST	United Nations Day				
6–7	GIVE US A CALL	Sweetest Day				
6–8	CELEBRATE WITH THE CLASSICS	Halloween				
6–9	TAKE A PERSONAL OPINION POLL	General Election Day				
6–10	COPY CAT	Veterans Day				
6–11	I'M THANKFUL FOR . . .	Thanksgiving Day				
6–12	RULES TO REMEMBER	Bill of Rights Day				
6–13	WRITE THE LYRICS	Forefathers' Day				
6–14	CHRISTMAS STEP PUZZLES	Christmas				
6–15	REARRANGE AULD LANG SYNE	New Year's Day				
6–16	WHO'S WHO?	Martin Luther King's Birthday				

Activity Number/Title		Skill Involved				
6-17	PATRIOTIC PARADE	Robert E. Lee's Birthday				
6-18	HAIL TO THE CHIEF	Inauguration Day				
6-19	MAKE A TOUCHDOWN	Super Bowl Sunday				
6-20	WHAT DO YOU SEE?	Groundhog Day				
6-21	LINCOLN'S DAYDREAM	Abraham Lincoln's Birthday				
6-22	SEND A LOVE-GRAM	Valentine's Day				
6-23	I CANNOT TELL A LIE	George Washington's Birthday				
6-24	SKIP IT	Leap Year Day				
6-25	WE'RE #1	"Music In Our Schools Month"				
6-26	SHAMROCK PUZZLE	St. Patrick's Day				
6-27	WHAT'S IN COMMON?	Easter				
6-28	WHAT HAPPENED THEN?	April Fool's Day				
6-29	FINISH THE TITLE	Arbor Day				
6-30	COMPOSER WORD SEARCH	Thomas Jefferson's Birthday				
6-31	HOW DOES IT LOOK?	Pan American Day				
6-32	YANKEE DOODLE	Patriots' Day				
6-33	SOLVE THE REBUS PUZZLES	San Jacinto Day				
6-34	DE COLORES (ALL IN COLOR)	May Day				
6-35	MOM'S MUSICAL CARD	Mother's Day				
6-36	REWRITE THE VERSE	Armed Forces Day				
6-37	TEST ON TAPS	Memorial Day				
6-38	WHAT COMES NEXT?	Flag Day				
6-39	A SINGING TELEGRAM	Father's Day				
6-40	DOT THE BATTLE HYMN	Independence Day				
6-41	PRESENT YOUR PICTURE	Friendship Day				
6-42	OUT OF THIS WORLD	National Aviation Day				

© 1987 by Parker Publishing Company, Inc.

Activity Number/Title		Skill Involved
Special Events		
6-43	MUSIC TERM REBUS	Field Day
6-44	POMP AND CIRCUMSTANCE	Graduation
6-45	CAN YOU PICTURE THAT?	Last Day of School
6-46	THANK-YOU GRAM	After a Field Trip
6-47	BEGIN HERE	Rehearsal Day
6-48	RAINY DAY PUZZLE	Rainy Day
6-49	FLASH BULLETIN	Musical Presentation
6-50	DESIGNING CONTEST	Musical Event

Name _____

Date _____

Craft Project for *Special Days Throughout the Year*

MUSIC ENVELOPE

Objective: The Music Envelope will be a useful item not only for this unit, but for the entire *Library*. This project adds interest in learning and encourages students to perfect their work and take pride in it.

Materials Needed:

- Copies of the envelope pattern
- Scissors
- Paste

Construction Directions:

1. Cut out the envelope pattern along the outside edges.
2. Fold the envelope on the dotted lines along the inside of the four flaps. Be sure the flaps all fold in the same direction. This will give you the shape of the envelope.
3. Put paste on the part of the two side flaps that cover the back of the envelope. When the paste is dry, the envelope is ready to use.

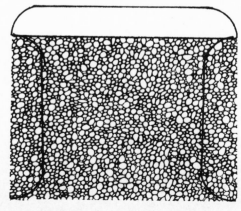

Uses: The Music Envelope was specifically designed for the delivery of the following activities in this unit:

> "A Note of Thanks"
>
> "Send a Love-Gram"
>
> "Mom's Musical Card"
>
> "A Singing Telegram"
>
> "Present Your Picture"
>
> "Thank-You Gram"

Once the envelope is constructed by cutting, folding, and pasting, this workshop atmosphere will be the starting point for creative thinking and originality. By self-discovery and self-expression, your students will probably think of most of these ideas on their own.

1. The envelope is a place for storing the Mini Music Flash Cards found in Unit 1, "Learning Music Theory." There are many activities throughout the *Library* that can use the envelope.

2. The envelope can be used to hand deliver or mail many music papers, special music activities, Share-a-Grams, and much more.

3. The Music Envelope can be traced on any type of paper and made in any color.

4. The envelope can be enlarged by changing the dimensions or using an opaque projector.

Incentive Badges

To the teacher: Cut apart badges and keep in a handy 3″ × 5″ file box along with tape. Encourage students to write their names and the date on the backs of their badges and to wear them.

MUSIC TOKEN

For hopping to it!
Good helper badge
in music class.

Watch OUT!

Best in the class . . . .
MUSIC AWARD

Creative WRITING

MUSIC CLASS AWARD

Great News

best   work

MUSIC AWARD

DOG GONE GOOD

MUSIC AWARD!

(name)

WELCOME

to
MUSIC CLASS

Congratulations!

creative drawing

MUSIC AWARD

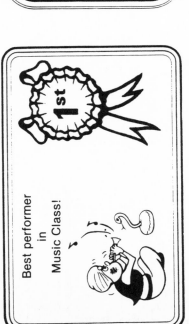

1st

Best performer
in
Music Class!

DON'T FORGET!

MUSIC

MUSIC SHARE-A-GRAM

TO: _____ DATE _____
            (Parent's Name)

FROM: _____ SCHOOL _____
        (Classroom Music Teacher)

RE: _____ CLASS _____
       (Student's Name)

To help you recognize your child's success in music class or any area that needs attention the following observation(s) has/have been made.

	Exceptional	Satisfactory	Unsatisfactory
Shows musical aptitude			
Shows creativity			
Shows talent			
Shows initiative			
Self-concept in music class			
Fairness in dealing with classmates			
Self-direction			
Care of instrument and equipment			
Reaction to constructive criticism			
Observes music class rules			
Starts and completes work on time			
Generally follows directions			

over for comments ▶

RETURN-A-GRAM

TO: _____ DATE _____
        (Classroom Music Teacher)

FROM: _____ SCHOOL _____
        (Parent's Name)

RE: _____ CLASS _____
       (Student's Name)

Please write your comments or questions on the back and return. If you want to be called for a parent-teacher conference, indicate below.

_____ Class _____ Year _____

(Student's Name)

STUDENT RECORD PROFILE CHART

Select the appropriate data in parentheses for each category, i, ii, iii, and iv, and record the information in the chart below as shown in the example.

i.—Unit Number for *Music Curriculum Activities Library* (1, 2, 3, 4, 5, 6, 7)

ii.—Date (Day/Month)

iii.—Semester (1, 2, 3, 4) or Summer School: Session 1 (S1), Session 2 (S2)

iv.—Score: Select one of the three grading systems, a., b., or c., that applies to your school progress report and/or applies to the specific activity.

a.

(O) = Outstanding
(G) = Good
(S) = Satisfactory
(NI) = Needs Improvement
(U) = Unsatisfactory
(I) = Incomplete
(—) = Absent

b.

(A) = 93–100 [percentage score]
(B) = 85–92
(C) = 75–84
(D) = 70–74
(F) = 0–69
(I) = Incomplete
(—) = Absent

c.

(R/P):
R = Correct number of responses.
P = Possible correct number of responses.
(I) = Incomplete
(—) = Absent

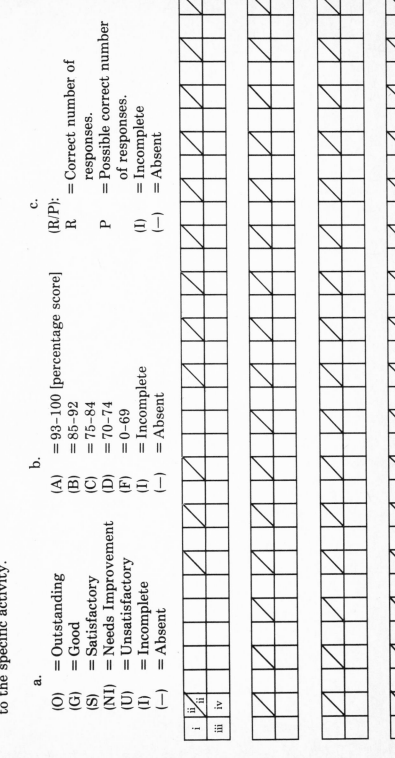

Student's Name _____ Class _____ Year _____

MUSIC SELF-IMPROVEMENT CHART (for student use)

a. On the back of this chart write your goal(s) for music class at the beginning of each semester.
b. On a separate sheet record the date and each new music skill you have acquired during the semester.

c. MUSIC SHARE-A-GRAM (date sent to parent)

d. RETURN-A-GRAM (date returned to teacher)

e. MUSIC AWARD BADGES (date and type rec'd)

1.
2.
3.

f. SPECIAL MUSIC RECOGNITION (date and type rec'd)

1.
2.
3.

g. SPECIAL MUSIC EVENT ATTENDANCE RECORD (date and name of special performance, recital, rehearsal, concert, field trip, film, workshop, seminar, institute, etc.)

1.
2.
3.
4.

h. ABOVE AND BEYOND: Extra Credit Projects (date and name of book report, classroom performance, construction of hand-made instrument, report on special music performance on TV, etc.)

1.
2.
3.
4.

i. PROGRESS REPORT/REPORT CARD RECORD (semester and grade received)

1.
2.
3.
4.

j. MUSIC SIGN-OUT RECORD (name of instrument, music, book or equipment with sign-out date and due date)

1.
2.
3.
4.
5.
6.
7.
8.
9.
10.